One Little Tooth

By Christine Economos
Illustrated by Pat Paris

Copyright © 2000 Metropolitan Teaching and Learning Company.
Published by Metropolitan Teaching and Learning Company.
Printed in the United States of America.

ISBN 1-58120-045-5

3 4 5 6 7 8 9 CL 03 02 01

"Marta, what are you doing?" asked Carlos.

"I'm brushing my teeth," said Marta. "I like to brush them. Do you see how white they are?"

"They look white. So what?" said Carlos.

2

"We're going to the dentist this morning," said Marta. "He is going to check our teeth. We have to rush or we'll be late."

"The dentist can't check my teeth," said Carlos. "I'm in a rush. I have a game this morning."

"We need to rush, Carlos," said Mama. "We don't want to be late."

"I wish I didn't have to miss my game," said Carlos. "And I wish I didn't have to go to the dentist. Just my bad luck. It makes me sick."

"Well, please don't be sick," said Mama. "Go and brush your teeth. They're a mess."

"I brush a lot," said Marta. "That is why my teeth are white. You should, too, Carlos."

"Pick, pick. All you do is pick," said Carlos.

"I'm going to check your teeth now, Marta," said Dr. Frank. "Are you brushing each day?"

"I never miss," said Marta.

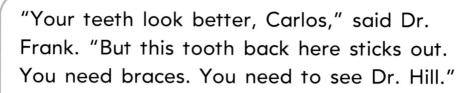

"Your teeth look better, Carlos," said Dr. Frank. "But this tooth back here sticks out. You need braces. You need to see Dr. Hill."

"Braces! We can leave the tooth the way it is," said Carlos. "Braces will mess me up."

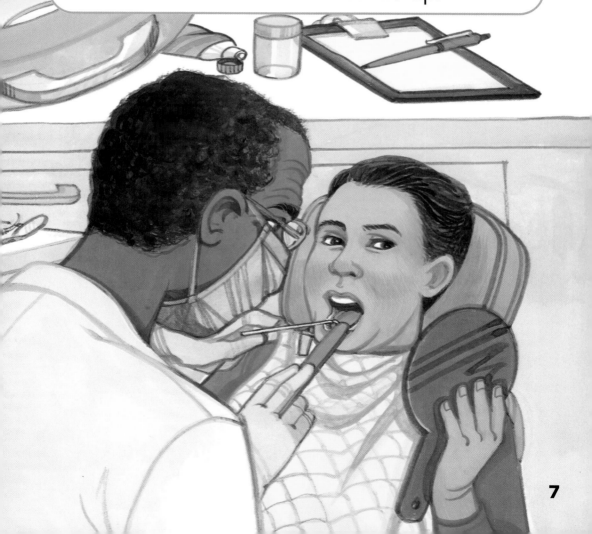

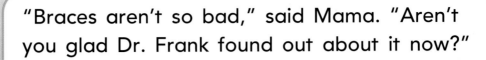

"Braces aren't so bad," said Mama. "Aren't you glad Dr. Frank found out about it now?"

"No! It's no big thing," said Carlos. "It's just one tooth. Please, Mama. Why do I need braces for just one little tooth?"

"I know it's a shock," said Mama. "But you can't leave the tooth the way it is. You would not want braces when you're old."

"This just isn't my day," said Carlos. "I miss my morning game and now this. What luck."

"Just one little tooth sticks out," said Carlos. "Now I need braces. Braces make me sick."

"I know it's a shock, Carlos," said Papa. "But braces aren't so bad. It will just be for a year or so."

"I have a tooth that sticks out a little," said Mama. "It has been that way for years. I wish I had had braces when I was a kid."

"What a mess," said Carlos. "I like this little tooth. I want to leave it the way it is."

"This morning I'll fit you for braces," said Dr. Hill. "You'll have them in a day or so."

"Isn't there another way?" asked Carlos. "I'm too old for braces. They'll mess me up."

"You're never too old," said Dr. Hill.

"I wish I had had braces," said Mama. "Then this tooth in back would not stick out."

"You have a tooth that sticks out?" asked Dr. Hill. "Why, I'll have to have a look."

"This may come as a shock," said Dr. Hill. "But you'll need braces for that tooth."

"Why? It's one little tooth. It isn't so bad," said Mama. "It just sticks out a little bit."

"A little bit too much," said Dr. Hill.

"But aren't braces just for kids?" asked Mama. "I like this tooth the way it is."

"Braces aren't just for kids," said Dr. Hill. "I'm glad I know about that tooth. What luck. We can fit you for braces, too."

"So you need braces, too," said Papa. "Just think what nice teeth you'll have."

"Aren't I too old for braces?" asked Mama.

"Please, Mama," said Carlos. "You're never too old for braces."